I0519018

Fun Snake Facts for Kids

Jacquelyn Elnor Johnson

www.CrimsonHillBooks.com

© 2024 Crimson Hill Books/Crimson Hill Products Inc.

All rights reserved worldwide. No part of this book, including words and illustrations, maybe be copied, lent for publication, excerpted, licensed, quoted nor used for artificial intelligence (AI) training. No robots nor any other form of AI were involved in any aspect of creating this work.

First edition, February 2024.

Cataloguing in Publication Data

Johnson, Jacquelyn Elnor

Fun Snake Facts for Kids

Description: Crimson Hill Books trade paperback edition | Nova Scotia, Canada

ISBN:	978-1-990887-76-5 (Paperback - Ingram)
BISAC:	JNF003000 Juvenile Fiction: Animals – General
	JNF003190 Juvenile Fiction: Animals – Reptiles & Amphibians
	JNF003170 Juvenile Nonfiction: Animals - Pets
THEMA:	PSVF - Zoology: amphibians & reptiles (herpetology)
	WNGS - Reptiles & amphibians as pets
	YNNM - Children's / Teenage general interest: Reptiles & amphibians

Record available at https://www.bac-lac.gc.ca/eng/Pages/home.aspx

Book design: Jesse Johnson

Crimson Hill Books
(a division of)
Crimson Hill Products Inc.
Lawrencetown, Nova Scotia
Canada

Crimson Hill
Books

They can be long, short, wide or thin.

They might be black, brown, orange, green, white or yellow.

They live almost everywhere in the world, so some of them probably live near where you do. Maybe right in your own back yard, like this harmless Garter Snake.

But you may never see them, and some of them can't see you. They're shy creatures, who'd rather live their secret lives...

Snake Fact:

Snakes don't fight to defend their own territories as most other animals do. Snakes don't have territories. They have a home area that they move around in, but other snakes will also live there. Their home area is where they know where to find water, shelter and food.

The Anaconda is one of the world's largest snakes. The other two in the top three biggest snakes are Pythons and Boa Constrictors.

What's so amazing about snakes?

Snakes live nearly everywhere in the world that people live.

There has never been a time in human history when there weren't snakes in the lakes, rivers, meadows, forests, mountains, plains, swamps, deserts and in the oceans that surround 6 of the world's 7 continents. The only continent that has no snakes, not even sea snakes, is Antarctica.

How many species of snakes are there? As far as we know (there may still be some humans have never seen) there are 3,789 species of snakes in the world. They are sorted into 30 families.

Most of the world's millions of snakes are completely harmless, preferring to live their lives far from human view. They are shy creatures who would rather slither away than attack. But about a third of snake species are more aggressive and dangerous than that. And about 40 species can attack and kill a human.

The most dangerous places to live in the world, if you're worried about dangerous snakes, are India, Africa and Australia.

Snakes can do many amazing things. All of them can swim and some live almost their entire lives in the water. Some can climb trees and launch themselves off branches to glide through the air. All of them can swallow prey that is much larger than they are.

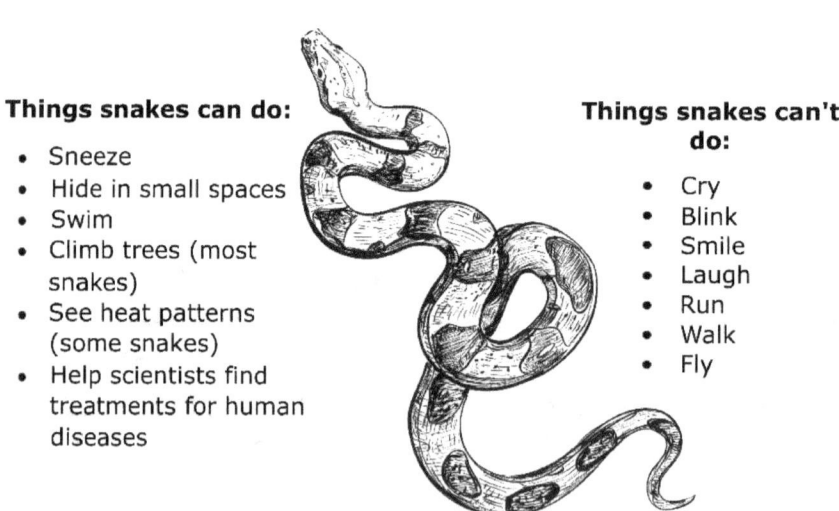

Things snakes can do:

- Sneeze
- Hide in small spaces
- Swim
- Climb trees (most snakes)
- See heat patterns (some snakes)
- Help scientists find treatments for human diseases

Things snakes can't do:

- Cry
- Blink
- Smile
- Laugh
- Run
- Walk
- Fly

This is a Corn Snake. They can make good pets.

Snakes are flexible and strong!

All snakes have long, strong and flexible bodies. This helps them move quickly when they want to, even though they don't have legs. They can only travel fast in short bursts, over short distances. Snakes are sprinters, not marathoners.

Snakes can use their strong muscles to move forward, backward or sideways.

All snakes are reptiles

All snakes are reptiles, but not all reptiles are snakes.

Reptiles are the group of animals that have scales. The reptile family includes lizards, crocodiles, turtles and tortoises, snakes, birds and the rare Taratua that lives only in New Zealand. They all have dry skin.

Most reptiles live on land, though some spend part or all of their lives in the ocean.

Reptiles are hard to know. Most of the them are shy. They prefer to live in a world without humans. Scientists have discovered that most reptiles just will not do their normal behavior when there are people around. This makes it harder for us to discover their secrets!

Most reptiles have their babies by laying eggs.

Like humans, snakes have a backbone and ribs as well as a skull. They have a heart, two lungs, a stomach and other organs inside their bodies similar to what humans have. They have skin under the scales that cover their bodies. They can see, hear, feel and smell things.

Some snakes have fangs.

Snake Fact:
In Ancient Greece people believed that all snakes are healers. You can still see the snake symbol for healing on many ambulances.

If this lizard had no legs, would you think it's a snake?

Are snakes amphibians?

Snakes are reptiles. Amphibians are a different group of animals.

All snakes have cool, dry skin covered in scales and they have no legs. They can live on land or in water, including lakes, rivers and the ocean. Most of them are land-dwellers.

Amphibians have wet skin and must live in or very close to water. Amphibians must return to water to lay their eggs. Most amphibians have legs. Toads, frogs and salamanders are all amphibians.

Reptiles are far older than dinosaurs!

Fish, other ocean animals, amphibians, reptiles, insects and mammals all existed before the dinosaurs appeared on earth. That was about 240 million years ago.

It was about 310 million years ago that the first reptiles lived. The first lizards evolved about 20 million years before the first dinosaurs did.

Snakes descended from one type of ancient lizard. This ancestor lizard had legs and was probably venomous. Other animals that came from this ancient lizard ancestor are Gila Monsters, Beaded Lizards, Monitor Lizards and Mosasaurs. Mosasaurs are an extinct ocean lizard that died out when the dinosaurs vanished from earth, about 65 to 66 million years ago.

Today, Beaded lizards live in Mexico and Guatemala. Gila Monsters live in Southwestern United States and Northwestern Mexico.

Monitor Lizards are much larger and their natural homes are in Africa, Asia, and Oceania, but one species has recently been found in the United States. It is an invasive species.

This means an animal that doesn't belong where it is and might have arrived on a shipping container. Or it could be an escaped pet that somehow was able to survive in its new home.

Mighty Titanoboa fights with a young T-Rex dinosaur. Titanoboa was a huge and probably ferocious snake, growing up to 42 feet or almost 23 metres long.

When did snakes first appear on earth?

The earliest known snake-like animals that we know of lived about 143 million to 167 million years ago. We know this because their fossils have been found by paleontologists (say this: pay-lee-on-tall-oh-jists). Paleontologists are the scientists who study ancient animals. The first true snakes lived about 112 to 94 million years ago.

Snakes probably first appeared on Earth during the Jurassic period, when dinosaurs dominated the Earth. These snake ancestor lizards might have lived in the water or on land, or both. They were probably venomous. This means they could stun or kill their prey with a poison their bodies made to do this. Some snakes today still have this ability to use venom.

There were snakes in the time of the dinosaurs, but it wasn't until the dinosaurs all died out, around 65 or 66 million years ago, that snakes changed to the many different types we know today.

Snake Fact:
Antivenin, also called antivenom, is the name for the treatment for a venomous snake bite. What type of antivenin is used to help a snakebite victim depends on what type of snake bit them.

This boy has a Reticulated Python. It won't try to eat him because it's well-fed.

The world's largest snake

While there are some awesomely large snakes in the modern world, none alive today is as big as Titanoboa.

The Green Anaconda is another big snake, up to 17 feet, or just over 5 metres long. The Anaconda is also the world's heaviest living snake. It can weigh more than 220 pounds, or almost 100 kilograms. The largest Anaconda ever found was 30 feet long. That's 9 metres! It was one big snake, 44 inches around its body, which is just over 1 metre! Anacondas are big enough to eat a wild pig or even an adult deer!

The largest known venomous snake is the King Cobra. There is one that lives at London Zoo in England that

A Reticulated Python can grow to be 23 feet long, or 7 metres!

is almost 19 feet long, or almost 6 metres. Left untreated, a King Cobra bite has strong enough venom to kill an adult Asian elephant.

Snake Fact:

Pythons are constrictors that can strangle a person in minutes and swallow them in less than an hour.

All snakes are covered in scales. Scales are like snake armor. It's there to protect their skin. Scales are lots of different shapes, including round, like this snake has. Scales are made of keratin. Human fingernails and hair are also keratin.

Snake Fact:
Most Sea Snakes prefer to stay in shallow water close to shore. However, when hunting, they can dive to 800 feet or 250 meters deep. The maximum depth an experienced scuba diver can go is 130 feet or 39.6 meters.

The Smallest snake is no longer than your middle finger!

The world's smallest snake is the Barbados Thread Snake. It got this name because it's not much wider than a piece of thread. Adults can grow to about as wide as a strand of spaghetti. This snake is just 4 inches or 10 centimetres long.

This tiny snake eats tiny food, the larvae of ants and also termites. In the wild, this little snake is critically endangered.

Snakes have no legs but a lot of ribs!

Like all mammals, including humans, snakes have a backbone. This backbone is made of connected bones called vertebrae. Connecting to each vertebra are ribs.

Adult humans have 24 vertebrae and 24 ribs, 12 on each side of their bodies. In humans, ribs protect the lungs and heart. Humans have 206 bones in their bodies.

Snakes have between 100 and 400 vertebrae. Each vertebrae has two ribs, meaning that the largest snakes can have 800 ribs! Snakes also have more bones than people do, about 300 to 400 for the largest snakes. Having a long body with so many bones helps snakes be strong and also very flexible.

Here's another close look at snake scales. These overlap and are shaped like leaves.

Once, snakes had legs!

There is no snake on earth today that has legs or feet. Yet all snakes had an ancient lizard ancestor that DID have legs and feet.

So how and why did snakes lose their legs? Scientists find it difficult to answer this question because snake skeletons are delicate. There are very few fossils of snakes. But here is what they think happened.

Some lizards, or maybe only one type of lizard, started to live more of its life underground in rock piles or crevices. This was to get away from enemies, or possibly this is where they hunted for other small creatures, like small mouse-sized mammals.

If this is what happened, it would be better not to have legs. It takes a lot of energy to have legs. Energy comes from food, so creatures with legs need to be able to find more food. Animals with no legs need less food to survive. Also, without any legs, snakes could fit into much smaller places, for example between rocks.

Snakes also wouldn't need ears and eardrums, so this could be why they also lost them, over many thousands of generations and millions of years.

Snakes aren't the only animal that has lost their legs as they evolved. Evolved means how an animal changes over time to adapt to new living conditions, such as climate change. Another animal that once had legs and no longer does is whales. Their very ancient ancestor lived on land but hunted for fish in the water. It had legs, feet, ears, nostrils and a long tail, all of which whales no longer have.

There are also other types of lizards that have lost their legs, like Glass Lizards. They look just like snakes, but they aren't snakes because, like other lizards, they have external ears (this means ears you can see on their heads) and they have eyelids.

Ground Skinks are lizards with tiny legs and feet. It could be that they are evolving now into animals that, perhaps thousands or millions of years in the future, will have no legs and look like snakes.

Snake Fact:

The longest Snake ever found was a Reticulated Python. It was 10 meters, or almost 33 feet long!

Snake Fact:
Large snakes can have as many as 1,200 bones.

This is a Black Mamba Snake.

Snake Fact:
Dozens of Sea Snake species live in the Pacific Ocean and Indian Ocean, but there are none in the Atlantic Ocean or the Caribbean.

Snake Fact:
Pythons crush their victims to death, so they don't have fangs, but they do have teeth. All their teeth are curved towards the back of their mouths. They can have as many as 80 teeth in 2 rows on the sides of their top and bottom jaw and another 2 rows of teeth in the middle of their top jaw. Their teeth are for holding onto their prey while they're attacking and killing them.

Where do snakes live?

If you were a snake, the most important thing in your life would be staying warm. But not too warm. Without any way to warm up your body, you'd have to depend on finding sunny spots to warm up. You'd also need to be able to get to cooler places to cool off, if you'd spent too long lying out in the sun.

For this reason, snakes need to live where it is warm most of the year, or where they can get to dens beneath the ground in cooler weather. They can't live in places that are always cold, which is why there are no snakes in Antarctica, but there are on every other continent in the world.

Where in the world are there no snakes?

There are no native snakes on some of the world's biggest islands. These islands are Ireland, Greenland, Iceland, all of the Hawaiian islands and New Zealand.

Even though New Zealand has no snakes on land, there are sea snakes in the ocean around its two islands.

There are also many smaller islands in the Atlantic and Pacific oceans that have no snakes. Cook Island, in the Pacific Ocean, does have an animal that you might think is a snake because that's what it looks like, but actually, it's a snake-eel. Even though it's easy to think they're snakes, snake-eels are fish.

There is one place in United States that is too cold for snakes. It also doesn't have any lizards or turtles in the lakes and rivers. It's Alaska, where the only reptile anyone has ever seen is sea turtles, and they are rare. There are also no native snakes in Hawaii.

There are no snakes in Antarctica and only one can live as far north as the edge of the Arctic Circle. That is the Common European Viper.

As Earth's climate gets warmer, it could be that snakes, like other animals, are able to find new homes in the Far North!

Where could a snake pet get you in trouble?

You'd be in big trouble if you got a snake for a pet in Hawaii or New Zealand. In both these places owning a snake is against the law!

It's different in Ireland, where you can have a pet snake, or see them at zoos, but there are no wild snakes, and never have been, because they can't survive in Ireland's cool, rainy climate.

If you want to live in Greenland with your pet snake, you can, but must get permission for your pet from the police.

Snake Fact:
Harmless Milk Snakes look a lot like Coral Snakes, whose venom can kill large animals and people.

This Garter Snake was born with two heads, a mistake that happens only once for every 100,000 snakes that are born.

World's largest snake party!

If you wanted to go to the world's largest snake party, do you know where you'd need to go?

It's Narcisse in Manitoba, Canada. That's about an hour and 20 minutes' drive away from Winnipeg. If you visit between the middle of April and the end of May, you will see a wonder of nature, the world's largest gathering of snakes. These are Garter Snakes. They spend the cold winter months in underground dens, brumating in great snake balls of hundreds, and in some dens thousands of snakes.

As the snows melt away and the weather warms, the snakes become active. The smaller males leave the dens first, gathering at the surface to wait for the females. When the females appear, there is a mating frenzy. There are walkways above the ground, where you can look down and see snakes covering the ground. At the peak of the season, there are 40,000 snakes tangled in great snake knots!

After mating, the snakes scatter to each find his or her own hunting territory, where they will live all summer and into the autumn. Males wander around, while females have live babies. The babies cluster around their mother for several hours after they're born, but she doesn't do anything to care for them. Instead, she wanders off, all her parenting duties done. The babies must fend for themselves.

As the weather cools in October, instinct tells these Garter Snakes to return to the winter protection of their dens.

The island owned by snakes

There is an island off the coast of Brazil that no one can visit because the residents have made it far too dangerous for humans to go there. It is Ilha da Queimada Grande, home to more than 4,000 Golden Lancehead Vipers, one of the world's most venomous snakes.

Because there are so many of these dangerous snakes on this small island, locals have called it Snake Island.

This is a Rat Snake with her eggs.

The Brazilian Navy has banned all visitors, leaving the island to its snake owners.

Snake Fact:

Millions of snakes died when snakeskin belts, shoes and handbags became fashionable. Though killing snakes to make them into luxury accessories is illegal today in many places, some snake species, like some Pythons, have become endangered because of poaching for the fashion industry.

Corn Snakes hatching.

Not ALL snakes lay eggs

Most snakes have their babies by laying eggs, but not all of them. The snakes that have live babies usually live in the cooler places. The reason snakes have learned to do this is that in cooler places, they can't rely on burying their eggs for the sun to keep warm until they hatch.

Depending on the species, a snake mother will lay 20 to 100 eggs. Live birth snakes usually have 10 to 20 babies, and sometimes as many as 30. Some large species of snakes can have more than that. Diamondback Water Snakes can have 40 babies at one time.

A Sleeping Python.

Some snake species can have their babies by parthenogenesis (say this: par-thin-oh-jen-iss-iss). This means the females don't need to mate to have babies. Two parthenogenesis snakes that live in United States are Copperheads and Cottonmouths.

Snakes sleep with their eyes wide open

With no eyelids, snakes can't ever close their eyes. They sleep with their eyes wide open, even though they are completely asleep. Usually they sleep coiled up, with their heads resting on their coils. When they

When snakes feel threatened, they have the ability to make the blood vessels in their eyes narrow. This temporarily makes their eyesight sharper, helping them escape. Temporarily means for a short time.

sleep, their breathing is slow and deep. Nobody knows if they dream when they're sleeping.

Snakes spend a lot of time sleeping. Most of them sleep for at least 16 hours a day, and some species sleep as much as 22 hours a day. Some snakes are night sleepers, like Corn Snakes and Garter Snakes, so they are awake during the day. You are less likely to see the snakes that prefer to sleep all day and hunt at night, like King Snakes.

What can snakes see?

Most snakes have only blurry vision. Some are blind. But snakes that live in trees or in water or hunt during the day usually have better eyesight than other species. The ones that live most of their lives underground, like Pine Snakes, have poor eyesight. Instead, they rely on their other senses to survive. Some snakes have evolved binocular vision.

Here's a way to easily tell a day-awake snake from one that prefers to hunt at night. The day snakes have round pupils in their eyes. The night stalkers have pupils that are shaped like slits.

Most snakes can't see the color red, even though their distant lizard ancestors probably could. Maybe long ago the snakes lost this ability when they moved underground.

They didn't need to see red, because nothing in their new world was red, so they lost this ability. A few sea snake species have evolved to get back their ability to see the color red.

Modern snakes can see blue and green in addition to black, white and gray. This is the same color range that dogs can see. Night-awake snakes have an extra seeing advantage because they can see ultraviolet light.

The only reason humans think that being able to see UV light is odd is that we don't have that ability (but there are some medical conditions that can cause a person to gain UV vision).

Many fish, amphibians, reptiles, birds, and some mammals are able to see UV light. They use it to help them find food or prey and find mates.

You can see this snake's nostril and eye are almost in a line on its head.

Snake breath!

Snakes have nostrils on their faces to breath, like other reptiles. They also have two lungs, but in snakes, one lung is large and it works, while the other one is very small and does not work.

The reason seems to be that snakes couldn't move quickly on their bellies and also breathe into two lungs at the same time.

For a long narrow creature that slithers on the ground and would rather flee than fight, one big lung just works better.

This Cerastes, or Desert Horned Viper, is a sidewinder. It lives in the Sahara Desert that covers most of Northern Africa.

How do snakes move?

Snakes slide along the ground on their bellies or swim in the water. They have 5 ways of doing this. These ways are:

1. **Lateral undulation** (say this: lat-ter-all un-due-lay-shun) – both land and sea snakes use this way of moving. To do it, a snake flexes its body to the left, then the right and keeps doing that, making its body move in waves. It relies on pushing against stones, rocks, twigs or soil. All snakes can use lateral undulation to move forwards, but only sea snakes can also use it to move backwards.

2. **Sidewinding** -- When there's nothing to push against because the snake is on a smooth surface like a sand dune or a mud flat, it might use sidewinding to get around. The snake looks like it is slipping and rolling sideways to move forward.

3. **Concertina** (say this: con-sir-teena) – When there's nothing to push against on the surface but no room for sidewinding, like in a tunnel, snakes use the concertina method. They place the lower part of their body against the tunnel wall and extend the front of their body. Then they pull their lower body forward, stopping and starting to go forward. This way of movement uses up a lot more energy than other ways, meaning snakes use it only when they have to.

4. **Rectilinear** (say this: wreck-ti-lyn-ee-er) – This is the slowest way snakes can move and is usually only used by the large snakes like Boas, Pythons and Vipers when they are stalking their prey. To move this way, a snake will lift its belly then place it down, pulling the rest of its body forward.

5. **A combination of all these ways of moving.** This is what snakes do when climbing trees. Snakes can move faster on small branches than on larger ones.

Snake Fact:

Most snakes have no venom. The ones that do almost always use it to weaken or kill their prey, not to defend themselves.

All sea snakes swim by making an S shape with their bodies and then pushing back and forth against the water.

Some Snakes have water-tight skin

Sea snakes have water-tight skin. This is what helps them float and allows them to swim. Some sea snakes also have a strange ability. They can breathe oxygen from the seawater through skin on their faces, between their nostrils and the tops of their heads.

This oxygen doesn't go to their lungs. Instead, it goes directly to their brains, allowing them to stay underwater for longer before they finally have to return to the surface to breathe air into their bodies.

Why do snakes hiss?

Snakes hiss to scare off predators, or to mark out their territory to other snakes, or because they've been disturbed while they're resting or sleeping. Hissing is a warning that they're about to attack.

Snake hissing is actually heavy breathing. Snakes do it by huffing air in and out of their mouths and noses.

The loudest hisser in the snake world is the Gopher Snake. It's hissing sounds like air escaping from a punctured car tire.

Flying snakes

Sounds like a horror film – snakes flying through the air, attacking when they land, but that's just a story. In real life, there aren't any snakes that can fly like most birds and some insects can do.

There is no snake that has wings, but some snakes have learned how to glide through the air. They do it by launching themselves from the tips of branches. In the air, they flatten their ribs out so there is air under their bodies and do a controlled fall through the air in a S shape, landing again on another tree. Depending on how high up in a tree they start their air acrobatics, gliding snakes can travel this way for as much as 300 feet, or 100 metres.

Though their flights only last a few seconds, while they're gliding snakes can go 25 miles per hour, or 40 kilometres per hour.

A snake eating a toad. Snakes can go months without a meal! They don't eat very often. Some snakes only eat 5 or 6 times a year. Others eat two, or maybe three meals a month.

It's only snakes that live in Southeast Asia that have ever been seen doing this. They can even do mid-air turns! What they can't do is attack anything while they're gliding or as they land.

Snake Fact:

Snakes that get good care and are protected from predators, like pets or snakes that live at a zoo or nature reserve, can live as long as 40 years. Most wild snakes usually live for only a few years.

Many snakes are excellent climbers. They do it by coiling their lower body and tail around a branch and extending their head upwards. Then they coil the first third of their body around a branch or tree trunk and pull their lower body upwards, and repeat. They are amazingly fast at climbing using this method.

What do snakes eat?

Snakes are meat-eaters. Snakes mainly eat small animals like mice, frogs, lizards, fish, snails, worms and the eggs or young of birds and small animals. Some snakes eat other snakes.

Wild snakes will only eat live prey.

Some snakes are stalking hunters. This means they search for their prey. Others are ambush hunters, waiting at a likely spot to catch an unwary victim.

When they do eat, it's always a big meal. Snakes usually hunt for an animal that is up to twice as large as their head. But some of the largest snakes have been seen eating animals that are much larger than that!

All snakes swallow their food whole

Snakes can't chew their food. They can't bite or tear their food into smaller chunks. They have to swallow it whole. The smaller snakes can only eat small animals, like rodents, insects or birds. The large snakes can eat larger animals, like crocodiles, deer, or pigs.

Snakes must rest after eating to digest their huge meals. If they are disturbed, they will throw up their meal, getting rid of the big bulge in their bellies so they can escape.

This Green Tree Snake isn't yawning, it's just rearranging its jaws. Snakes can open their mouths twice as wide as their heads! No human could ever do this.

Open wide!

Snakes can open their mouths really wide because they have a flexible skull. Snakes can make their jaws bigger to swallow, something that no other animal can do.

Snakes have teeth. They just don't use them to chew. Instead, their teeth are curved back towards their throats. They use their teeth to keep their prey from escaping.

Some snakes can eat an egg whole. Spikes on their backbones break up the eggshell. Snakes can't digest

This Grass Snake is taste-smelling the air with its very sensitive tongue. Most snakes can't see very well. They use their tongues to find their prey.

eggshells, so egg-eating snakes throw up the shell pieces to get rid of them.

Can snakes yawn?

When snakes open their mouths wide, they look like they're yawning. But they're not doing it because they're tired! When snakes open their mouths like this, stretching their jaws very wide, what they're doing is mouth gaping. We're still not sure why they gape, but it may be just that they want to stretch out their muscles and get their faces rearranged.

How do snakes find their prey?

Prey means the animals they eat. Most snakes don't have very good eye-sight. Some snakes are blind. Snakes also aren't very good at hearing things. What they do have is an incredible sense of smell, but not because of their noses. Snakes only use their noses to breathe.

Snakes use their tongues to taste and understand their world. Every snake's tongue is forked, with two prongs. The prongs are called tines. Snakes open their mouths, stick out their tongues and sweep the air with their tines. What they are doing is picking up tiny molecules of odors, from two different places at the same time on their two tines. This means they're smelling in stereo!

By moving around, this tells them what direction the smell is coming from. They pull their tongue back into their mouth, touching the tine tips to the Jacobson's organ. This organ is on the roof of their mouth at the back and connects directly to their brain. This is how they know what they're smelling and what direction to go in to find it (if it is prey) or avoid it (an enemy).

Snakes can't hear the high-pitched squeaks of a mouse, like a cat can. But they can taste that mouse's scent and find it because of their forked tongues!

Snake Fact:

Only some Snake species have teeth. In the ones that do, their teeth are always curved backwards towards the back of the mouths.

This is a Blue Viper. All Vipers are venomous.

Smells that snakes hate

There are some odors that snakes will do anything to avoid. These are anything that is a very strong smell, or it is spicy, or bitter.

Snakes don't like the smells of bleach, sulfur, vinegar or cinnamon. Like all animals, they are afraid of fire and hate the smell of smoke.

Snake Fact:
Most snake bites happen when someone is trying to catch a snake or kill it.

What can snakes taste?

Snakes can't taste their food. They eat when they're hungry. They don't have any taste buds in their tongues or mouths.

Do snakes poop?

Just like us, snakes have to poop after they eat. Their poop is everything they couldn't digest. This includes the hair, claws or feathers of their prey.

It's brown and stinky. The white stuff in their poop is their pee.

Snakes can also fart!

What can snakes hear?

Snakes don't have ears on the outside of their heads like mammals have. But they do have small ear holes on the sides of their heads. These ear openings lead to an inner ear, but snakes' inner ears have no eardrums. This means that snakes can hear some sounds, but not very well.

Instead, they depend on ground vibrations. Their inner ear bones are connected to their jawbones, and this helps them feel vibrations. But their main vibration-detector is their sensitive bellies. They know when another animal is coming towards them by the faint vibrations that animal is making as it moves.

This is a Yellow Viper.

Can snakes feel pain?

Injured snakes do feel pain. Even when their head is cut off, a snake's body will still be alive, and in pain, for about an hour before it finally dies.

Are snakes smart?

Snakes, like all animals, are as smart as they need to be to stay alive in their world. This means they know how to find food, water, shelter and a mate so that their species will survive into the future.

Scientists have discovered that some snakes can do more than this, though few snakes have been tested for intelligence. Ball pythons are one that has, and they've shown that they can recognize people they know, like their owners if they're pets.

Other researchers have discovered that the snakes they studied were able to remember things that happened and change their behavior to match what they've learned. We also know that snakes choose a place to ambush their prey, like mice, because they can smell that another snake recently caught something and ate it there.

Timber Rattlesnakes can follow the scent trail of another snake out of a maze.

Snakes can use their memories to tell them what other animals are dangerous to them, and which ones aren't. Or what animal is prey, and what ones to avoid.

What snakes (and all reptiles) don't have is brains that understand emotions, like happy, sad, angry, or being bored.

Snake Fact:

The mongoose, a small animal that lives in Southern Europe and Asia, attacks and eats venomous snakes. Mongooses are immune to snake venom. In a mongoose-Cobra standoff, the mongoose will usually win.

This is an Eastern Hognose Snake.

Playing dead

Some snakes play dead when they are threatened by an enemy. One is the Eastern Hognose Snake. It lives in Georgia, United States. When it's in danger, it will roll on its back, open its mouth, and play dead until the enemy goes away. This is why some people call the Eastern Hognose a zombie snake.

Other snakes that sometimes play dead to fool their enemies are Corn Snakes and European Grass Snakes.

Snake Fact:

The world's most endangered snake is the St. Lucia Racer. No one is sure how many there still are, but experts agree there are less than 100 left in the West Indies.

Snakes sleep with their eyes wide open. They might look like they're awake, but they're completely asleep. Some snakes sleep for up to 22 hours a day.

Do snakes hibernate in the cold months of the year?

Snakes, like most other reptiles (except birds) and amphibians, don't hibernate to survive when it's cold out. Animals that hibernate are actually asleep. Instead, snakes and other reptiles and amphibians become very still, even though they are still awake. This cold weather stillness is called brumation (say this: BREW - may-shun).

When snakes are brumating, they might look like they're dead, but their eyes are open. They have slowed down how often their heart beats as their body cools and they breathe less often than normally, even though they are awake.

Snakes choose safe places to brumate, like caves, under rock piles or inside fallen trees. Some species, like garter snakes, brumate together in large numbers that clump together.

Before they go into brumation, snakes must eat to have enough energy to get through brumation. It can last up to eight months.

As the weather gets warmer, the snakes will slowly warm up, become active and head from their hidden winter homes to the surface to mate. Then they scatter to find their own territories and hunt for the first meal they've had for months.

Snake Fact:
Snakes can sneeze. They usually do it when they're about to shed or they have a cold.

This is a shed snakeskin. Snakes, like some other reptiles, shed their skins when they get too tight to continue growing and to get rid of parasites.

Why snakes' eyes sometimes turn blue

Snakes' eyes start to look cloudy and change color to bluish gray when they are about to shed their skin. This happens because snakes need to shed their scales and skin to allow them to grow and to keep their skin healthy. They have scales all over their bodies, including covering their eyes.

After shedding, snakes' eyes go back to their normal colors. Some snakes have yellow, green or red eyes, but most have eyes that are black.

Snakes have to shed their skin

Snakes usually shed their skins several times a year. Some young snakes are growing so fast they shed every month. Shedding also helps snakes get rid of bacteria or parasites like mites and ticks in their skin that they've picked up from the ground.

Before shedding, snakes stop eating. They find a place to hide where they feel safe.

When they're ready to shed, their skin probably feels itchy. They rub against the ground, a rock or a tree. The old skin breaks away, starting at their mouth. Very slowly, they slither out of their old skin.

The skin comes off inside-out. It usually takes a few days for a snake to get rid of its old skin.

Their new skin is larger and the colors are brighter. When a snake sheds, it also sheds the scales that cover and protect its eyes. Then it grows new eye scales.

Very young snakes need to shed as often as four times a year. Adult snakes usually only need to shed twice a year.

Most snakes are harmless!

Though many people are afraid of snakes, most snakes are completely harmless to people. More Americans die each year from bee stings or wasp stings than from snake bites.

This Red-Bellied Black Snake is venomous. It lives in Eastern Australia.

Snakes aren't poisonous

Snakes aren't poisonous because a poison is something that that is eaten or breathed in. Venom is something that is injected into a victim by a bite. This is why dangerous snakes are venomous, not poisonous.

Snake country!

Most snakes don't have any venom. Of the ones that do, most don't have venom strong enough to kill a human. But there are snakes that are deadly for

This is a Bush Viper showing off its fangs. Bush Vipers live in Africa.

people. The most snakebite deaths each year happen in India. The next most dangerous snake countries are in Western Africa and Australia.

If you love snakes, you might want to visit Australia. It's the country with the most snake species in the world.

Dangerous snakes!

Of the thousands of snake species, about 200 species can kill a human with one bite. Cobras, Vipers and Sea Snakes are the most dangerous of the venomous snakes.

An Emperor Brown Snake. It lives in Australia.

All snakes that are venomous are unpredictable. They can go from coiled and resting to attacking in seconds. They are also aggressive and able to move quickly.

The world's most venomous snake is the Inland Taipan. Just one bite from this dangerous snake has enough venom to kill 100 people, or 250,000 mice. Scientists can't explain why the Inland Taipan has developed such a powerful venom that is so much stronger than it needs to survive.

Venom is snake saliva. When they bite, it doesn't come from their mouth, but from their fangs which are connected to venom glands in their head.

Snakes are immune to their own venom. So are some birds and mammals that are their prey. They've adapted to protect themselves from snake attacks. King Snakes are harmless, but they eat venomous snakes. King snakes have also evolved to be immune to the venom of their prey.

G'day, mate – Australian Snakes

The most dangerous Australian snakes are the Inland Taipan and the Eastern Brown Snake.

Someone who is bitten by an Inland Taipan and doesn't immediately get anti-venom will die, usually in less than 45 minutes.

The Eastern Brown Snake's science name is Pseudonaja, meaning "false Cobra." It gets this name because it raises its body and flattens it, like a true Cobra, before striking. Despite their name, they can be brown, very pale brown, black or even orange. This color variety is common among Australian snakes, making identifying them more difficult.

Even though Australia has so many venomous snakes, only about five deaths from snake bites happen there each year. In Australia you are more likely to die because of a bee sting or in an accident with a horse than by snake bite.

Snake Fact:
Western Garter Snakes live in U.S. and have no scales. Like all Garter Snakes, the Western Garter Snake has live babies.

This is a Yellow White-Lipped Viper showing how strong all snakes are. It lives in Southeast Asia.

Sea Snakes have flat tails to help them swim.

Indian and African Snakes

The Saw-Scaled Viper is the world's most deadly snake. There are snakes whose venom is stronger, but this snake kills more people each year than any other snake because it is the most aggressive. It is quick to strike and bites several times when it attacks.

It lives in Africa and Southwestern Asia, including India and Sri Lanka. It isn't a large snake, usually only up to 3 feet, or 1 metre long.

Traditionally, snakes were worshipped as gods by many people in India and this is still true today. There are many temples devoted to Cobras in India.

All Sea Snakes Are Venomous!

Most of the 70 species of sea snakes live in the warmest parts of the Pacific Ocean and in the Indian Ocean. They like to live in shallow water, especially near coral reefs.

All sea snakes have a flat tail that helps them swim. They also can close their nostrils (that's the nose opening) when they're underwater.

Sea snakes have big lungs, so they can stay underwater a long time. They can also 'breathe' through the skin on their faces, getting oxygen from the water through their skin.

Some snakes can stay underwater for up to two hours before they need to come back to the surface to breathe!

Usually, sea snakes use their venom on fish, but it can be dangerous for humans. A Beaked Sea Snake has enough venom to kill 50 people in one bite.

This snake is a Palm Pit Viper.

Pit Vipers

Pit Vipers didn't get their name because they live in holes in the ground or old mining pits. Instead, they're members of a group of snakes that have pits on their heads. These pits allow them to see heat patterns of prey, like the heat a mouse's body is giving off.

Pit Vipers live in Europe, Asia, North America and South America. They have two heat-sensing pits between their eye and nostril on each side of their heads.

There are 151 species of Pit Vipers, including Rattlesnakes, Asian Pit Vipers and Lanceheads.

The most dangerous snakes in United States

If you want to visit the place with the most snakes in United States, you need to go to Texas. But if you'd rather have a vacation where there are the most dangerous snakes, you'll need to go to Arizona. 19 of the 21 venomous snakes in United States live there.

The most dangerous snakes in United States are the Coral Snake, Copperhead, Cottonmouth and the several types of Rattlesnakes. The Yellow-Bellied Sea Snake is also venomous.

In the entire world there are millions of people bitten by snakes each year. More than 100,000 people die each year from the venom in these bites. Most of these people could have survived if they'd gotten antivenom medicine in time.

In the United States, there are less than 2,000 snake bites each year and only 8 to 10 people die of snakebites.

Snake Fact:

The longest snake in United States is the Eastern Indigo Snake. Despite its name, it isn't blue. It's black and lives in southeastern United States. Eastern Indigo Snakes can grow to be 9 feet, or 274 centimeters long.

There are several types of Rattlesnakes in North America. Some have diamond shaped patterns, others are brown, black and cream. All of them have rattles at the ends of their tails.

Rattlesnakes

The largest venomous snake in Untied States is the Eastern Diamondback Rattlesnake. Its fangs can be an inch, or 2.5 centimetres long! It mostly hunts for rabbits. It lives in Southeastern United States. Like all Rattlesnakes, it can strike without using its rattles.

The Western Rattlesnake is the most aggressive of all Rattlers.

Rattlesnakes' rattles are actually rows of hollow scales that are only loosely connected to their tails. When

You can tell Coral Snakes by their bright colors of black and red with yellow rings. They are night-hunters, so seldom seen in daylight.

they shake their tails, a sign that they're about to attack, the scales rattle, making a buzzing sound.

Some herpetologists (say this: herp-pet-tall-oh-jists) believe that Rattlesnakes can't hear the rattling sounds they're making. Herpetologist is the name for scientists who study snakes.

Coral Snakes

It's wise to avoid Coral Snakes because there is no antivenin (the medicine to reverse venom) available today. Fortunately, of the 100 or so Coral Snake bites of humans in North America each year, almost all of these bites contained too little venom to kill a human.

This is a Southern Copperhead.

Copperheads

The Copperhead is a venomous snake that lives in Eastern United States and also in Mexico.

Copperheads can be hard to see because they freeze when they see a human. This can make it easier to accidentally step on them and get bitten!

The first bite will contain no venom. It's just a warning bite. If the Copperhead still feels threatened, it will bite again and the second bite always includes venom.

Like all other snakebites, a Copperhead bite can be painful. But with this snake, the bite is rarely deadly.

Snake Fact:

Venomous snakes are immune to their own venom.

A Cottonmouth about to strike.

Cottonmouths

Cottonmouths are also called Water Moccasins because they live in swamps, creeks or rivers. They are only found in Southeastern United States.

The Cottonmouth gets its name from its white mouth. When threatened, it will open its mouth very wide and hiss.

The Cottonmouth is the only snake in the world that lives both in water and on land. It can also live in the ocean. This has allowed this snake to colonize offshore small islands.

Snake Fact:
Snakes breathe with their noses but they smell things with their tongues.

Yellow-bellied Sea Snake

This snake is more comfortable in warm water than on land. It lives in the Pacific Ocean, from as far north as Washington state to South America. It also lives in the Indian Ocean.

It does not like fresh water (that's lakes or rivers) and lives entirely on fish.

Dangerous Snakes – Canada and Mexico

There are only four snakes that are venomous and live in Canada. They are Western Rattlesnakes that live in British Columbia, Prairie Rattlesnakes in Saskatchewan and Alberta, Massasauga Rattlesnakes in Ontario and the rare Desert Nightsnake. It lives only in one part of British Columbia. Of these, the three Rattlesnakes are the ones that can kill humans.

In Mexico, the snakes to be wary of are the Vipers, Coral Snakes, Colubrids and Sea Snakes. The King Snake is a Colubrid. The Western Diamondback Rattlesnake is the species that causes the most snakebite deaths in Mexico each year.

Snake Fact:
Snakes need to drink water. They don't lap it up with their tongues. Instead, they drink with their mouths, like people do.

This is the Comon European Viper, also called the Adder in Great Britain. It is the only snake that can live as far north in the world as the edge of the Arctic Circle.

The Adders of England, Scotland and Wales

Compared to other places in the world, snakes have become fairly rare in Great Britain. There are only three snake species in England and Wales. They are harmless Grass Snakes and Smooth Snakes and the venomous Adders. Only the Adders live in Scotland.

There are fewer snakes than there used to be in Great Britain, mainly because of competition for places to live. As humans need more land for farming and houses, the snakes, like other wildlife, are being pushed out of their territories.

This is a pet ball python.

Snakes in Japan

Of the 47 snake species that live in Japan, 4 are venomous. The most dangerous is Mamushi, or the Japanese Viper, a type of pit viper. Mamushis bite between 2,000 and 4,000 people each year, and the bite causes them to be seriously ill, but they usually recover. There are about 10 Mamushi bite deaths per year for all of Japan.

Japan has one of the strangest venomous snakes, the Yamakagashi. It can't make its own venom. Instead, it hunts for poisonous frogs, eats them, then stores their toxins in glands in the skin of its neck to use on its own prey, including humans. A Yamakagashi bite, if not treated, causes a victim to bleed to death.

A Green Mamba's venom works very quickly on the nervous system of their victims. A person who is bitten by a Green Mamba needs immediate medical help or they could die.

Green Mamba

Green Mambas are one tricky snake. They can go from being calm to being angry and aggressive in a flash, and then they strike over and over. They are fast, very agile and like to live in trees.

Green Mambas live near the ocean in southern Africa. This includes South Africa, Kenya, Mozambique, Tanzania, Eastern Zimbabwe and Southern Malawi.

Snake Fact:
Harmless Garter Snakes have no fangs, but they do have venom they use it to stun their prey.

Black Mambas are the longest poisonous snakes in Africa, growing to be 14 feet or about 4 and a half metres long. They are an inland snake, living in the rocky hills and on the savannas of southern and eastern Africa.

Black Mamba

You might wonder about the name of this snake, because its skin is dark greenish-gray, not black.

But if you were near a Black Mamba when it showed the part of its body that is black, you'd be in terrible danger. When a Black Mamba opens its black mouth wide, hisses and sticks out its long black tongue, it's about to attack!

They strike and bite not just once, but many times.

A person who is bitten by a Black Mamba and doesn't have any anti-venin medicine with them will die in about 20 minutes.

Don't think you would be able to just run away. Black Mambas can slither at 12.5 miles per hour (or 20 km per hour) in sprints on level ground. This makes them the world's fastest snake!

Some athletes can run this fast. Most people can't without a lot of training.

Mangrove Snake

Mangrove snakes, also called Cat Snakes, live in Southeast Asia. They are mildly venomous and are black with gold rings around their bodies.

There is also a Mangrove Sea Snake that lives in Australia.

Snake Fact:
In the Maya and Aztec calendars, the fifth day of the week is called Snake Day.

Snake Fact:
Chameleon Snakes are the only Snakes we know of that can change their color to match the ground or leaves they are on. This helps them hide from their predators. They live in Madagascar, an island nation east of Africa.

Green Tree Pythons dangle their tails to attract any curious creature, then wrap their tails around a branch and hang from it to capture the unwary prey.

Green Tree Pythons

They're called Green Tree Pythons, but that doesn't mean they're always green! This snake is always brightly colored, but they could be red, blue, yellow or black. Sometimes they are even white! Not only that, they change colors, depending on how old they are and their hormones. Their colors change throughout their lives.

Even though, like all snakes, Pythons are cold-blooded, they are the only snakes that can warm up their eggs. They do it by coiling around them, then twitching their muscles to raise or lower their own temperature. They can use their heat pits to check how warm the eggs are, and either do some more twitching to warm them up, or stay still to cool them off.

Green Tree Pythons live in New Guinea, Indonesia and Australia.

Cobras

Cobras can spit venom when they raise their bodies off the ground and blow up their necks to create a hood. They control their hoods with their rib muscles. Usually, when hooding and spitting venom, they're also hissing at their enemy.

Cobras live in southern Africa, southern Asia and islands near southeast Asia.

Cobras females are the only snake species we know of that always makes a nest for her eggs.

This is a King Cobra. All Cobras can raise as much as one-fifth of their total length in a 'standing up' position when they face off against an enemy.

King Cobra

This snake lives in South and Southeast Asia. It mostly lives in swamps or forests and eats small mammals, lizards and birds. It can grow to be 18 feet, or almost 5 and a half metres long.

They are 1 of only 2 species of snake that make a nest for their eggs. In their lives, they never stop growing. They must shed their old skins five times a year. This means that a snake that lives to age 20 will shed its skin 100 times!

Snake charmers and their captive Cobras in India.

Snakes have poor hearing, so we don't know if Cobras can actually hear the tunes that snake charmers play on their flutes, which in India are called pungi, or been, or bin. Snakes can hear lower frequency sounds through their ears, so it might be they hear the low notes, or just the male voices of the snake charmers.

Or possibly they're just curious about what's going on when someone lifts the lid of the baskets where they're coiled and waiting for something interesting to turn up. Like a juicy mouse, maybe.

Snake charming has been against the law in India since the 1970s because it was judged to be animal cruelty.

Boa Constrictors squeeze their victims to death.

Boa Constrictor

As Boa Constrictors tighten their bodies around prey, they can sense their dying victim's heart rate. This tells the snake how much pressure to apply and when to stop squeezing.

Boas live from Northern Mexico to Argentina.

If a Boa ever wound itself around you, the best way to get it off your body is for someone else to unwind it, starting with the tail.

Snake Fact:
A Snake's fangs wear out quickly. Snakes shed their fangs every 6 to 10 weeks and grow new ones.

Anacondas live in South America.

Green Anaconda

A Green Anaconda can eat a deer, wild pig, jaguar or caiman.

A native of South America, Anacondas are the world's largest living snake. They live in swamps and slow-moving rivers in the Amazon and Orinoco River basins in South America.

Recently, some have been spotted near Miami in Florida. They are probably pets that have been abandoned by careless pet owners.

Green Anacondas are constrictors who squeeze their prey to death.

Snake Fact:
A scientist who studies Snakes is called an Ophiologist.

This is a pet corn snake.

Rat Snakes

Rat snakes are group of large constrictors that look dangerous and can bite but are completely harmless unless you're a chicken. Or a rat.

Rat Snakes live in Asia, Europe and also in eastern North America from Ontario to Texas and Florida. They can be gray, brown, green, yellowish-orange or yellowish-white. Some, like the Mandarin Rat Snake, have patterns.

At 190 centimeters or just more than 6 feet long, Rat Snakes are the largest snake in Canada. They lay their eggs in piles of leaves.

Corn Snakes, one type of Rat Snake, are popular as pets.

This is a Speckled Rattlesnake. It lives in Southwestern United States and Northern Mexico.

Protect yourself!

If you are ever threatened by a snake, calmly back away.

If you are ever bitten by a snake, don't try to catch it or kill it, but you do need to remember what it looks like. Get IMMEDIATE medical help. You might need the anti-venom, which all hospital emergency departments have.

Each snake species has different venom. This is why you need to tell caregivers what the snake looked like so they know which anti-venom will work to help you.

Snakes on a plate!

Snakes are considered a delicacy in some Asian countries, including Taiwan, Thailand and China, where many people are fond of snake soup in the colder months. Cobra and Water Snake meat are also used in stir-fries and stews.

If you'd like a taste of snake, there is one place in United States where Rattlesnake is often on the menu. That's Texas, where there are 10 species of Rattlesnakes. If you go to Sweetwater Rattlesnake Roundup State Championship Cook Off, held each year in March, you too could wrap your lips around a tasty Texan Rattlesnake dinner.

Snake invaders!

Some snakes live where they don't belong. They might have escaped from zoos or nature sanctuaries. Or they might have been abandoned pets released into the wild when their owners could no longer care for them.

Most pets can't survive in the wild. They've never learned to fend for themselves. But some not only survive, they thrive, because in their new habitat they can find shelter and plenty of food. There may be no natural enemies in their new home.

This is what happened with the Burmese Pythons that shouldn't live in Florida, but they do, in Everglades National Park. They compete with the native animals

Most pythons don't make good pets.

for food and are blamed for wiping out some of the native birds, mammals and other reptiles.

This is seriously bad news, and not just for the Pythons' food competitors or prey. It means the whole biosystem in the park is changed. Since the Pythons arrived, raccoons, opossums and bobcats have nearly disappeared in the park. Rabbits and foxes are completely gone. No humans have died from the Burmese Pythons, but it could happen.

Once an invasive species has spread it is very difficult, and usually impossible, to get rid of them. While no one knows exactly how many Pythons there are in Florida, experts say it is probably tens of thousands in the Everglades alone. Pythons have also been seen in the Florida Keys and near Miami.

In Australia, Wolf Snakes arrived on Christmas Island in 1987. Since then, this venomous snake has destroyed the native reptile population, wiping out the skinks and geckos. Four of the island's lizard species are now extinct. Before the Wolf Snakes arrived, there were no snakes on the island, and the native species had no way to defend themselves from snakes.

The Brown Tree Snake has done the same on the island of Guam. It accidentally arrived there as a stowaway on an American military plane in the 1940s. Because the Brown Tree Snakes have been so successful as newcomers to Guam, 10 of Guam's 12 native forest birds are now extinct. Killed by the snakes, most of the bats are gone and so are half of Guam's native reptiles.

Snakes escaping where they don't belong upsets the local natural order and reduces biodiversity. It's bad for that area and, usually, not so good for the snakes either. Eventually, people hunt them down, capture them and kill them, trying to protect the native species of birds, other reptiles and mammals, and maybe also humans if the invaders are venomous.

Snakes that can be pets

The ancestors of Florida's two worst invasive snakes, Pythons and Boa Constrictors, first came to the state as pets. About 100,000 Burmese Pythons were imported into United States between 1996 and 2006. When their owners discovered how huge these snakes can get, how much they eat and how scary they can

A pet King Snake.

be, they just let them go. Pythons and Boas have been banned as a pet in Florida since 2012.

Not only did these snakes get really big and need a lot of food, they became known for attacking their owners or family members. But there are a few, much smaller, safer and gentler snakes that are bred in captivity to be good pets. The two best pet choices if you want a snake are Corn Snakes and Milk Snakes.

Corn Snakes, their owners report, are easy pets to please, always docile and gentle. They love to burrow in their vivariums. Corn Snakes are nocturnal, meaning they sleep during the day and are awake at night.

Milk Snakes are a sub-group of King Snakes. They can be white with orange rings or black with orange and gold rings. They are easy to care for and usually docile as pets.

All the pets you buy from a pet snake breeder are captive bred. This means their parents and grandparents were bred to be pets and they have learned to live happily as pets. Catching wild snakes, like Garter Snakes for example, because you hope they can be a pet is never a good idea. They are wild and prefer their wild lives. They do not know how to be good pets, and don't want to be.

Are snakes endangered?

As humans, we need to protect our snakes. They are a part of our beautiful, natural world. They help to control pest animals that can spread disease, such as mice and rats. They have their place in each ecosystem where they live.

It could be that, because of snakes, one day we will be able to help many people live longer, healthier lives.

Some snakes, like many animals, are threatened by shrinking habitats. They're being pushed out of their home territories by other animals or, most often, by humans.

Very few snakes are endangered. Some are thriving with climate change. It means that they may be able to live further north in the Northern Hemisphere, or further south in the Southern Hemisphere, as these places become a bit warmer.

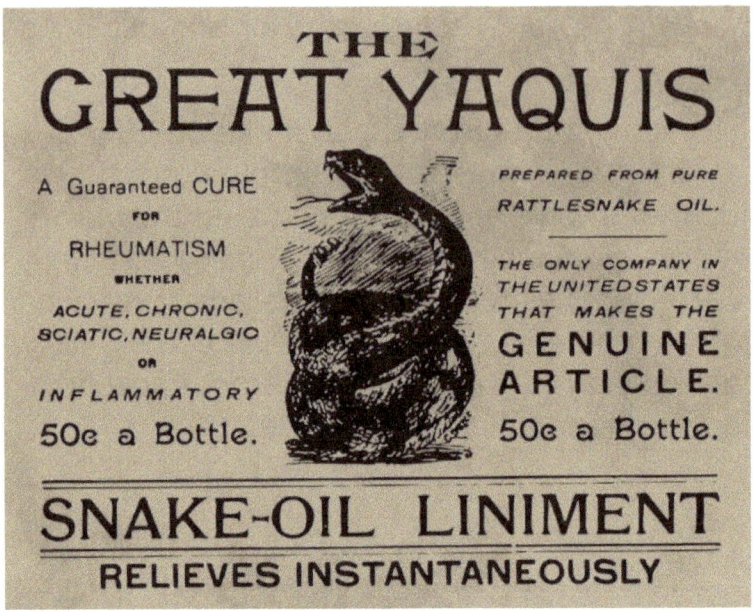

Snake Oil was a term used for mostly useless health remedies sold by travelling salesmen in the 1800s.

Milking a snake to get their venom. Scientists are looking for ways to use snake venom to make medicines for people who have cancer, heart disease and other illnesses.

Could snakes help cure humans?

Humans have long suspected that snake venom could in some way improve their health. Various strange mixtures were sold, claiming to cure everything from cramps or headaches to arthritis and even cancer.

Unfortunately, all these Snake Oils usually did was give people false hope and help the people who sold these worthless products get rich. As a result, people started calling fake medicines "snake oil."

However, it seems snake venom actually could help cure some serious human health issues, scientists are now discovering. It is snake venom that is used to make anti-venom for snake bites. It also might help people with cancer or who are paralyzed.

Right now, several elements in snake venom are being researched and might one day be treatments that work for cancer, arthritis, strokes, heart disease, hemophilia, to lessen pain and control bleeding during surgery.

Snake Fact:
All Sea Snakes need to drink fresh water. They cannot drink sea water. Some head to land to find water to drink. Others wait until it rains and drink the fresh rainwater on the surface of the ocean.

Thank you!

I hope you've enjoyed reading this book of strange and amazing facts about snakes.

If you want to know more about the world's most fascinating and fantastic creatures, including some that make great pets, turn the page!

Best wishes,

Jacquelyn

About Jacquelyn

Jacquelyn Elnor Johnson started telling stories to entertain her younger sisters, discovering in the telling what it takes to engage your audience! By age 15, she was a correspondent for the local newspaper and had written her first book. She went on to have careers in writing for and editing newspapers and magazines and teaching journalism.

A life-long pet lover, she is the bestselling author of 19 books about caring for and enjoying pets and animals.

In addition to writing practical, helpful and entertaining non-fiction for kids in grades 3 to 7, she writes novels including the Morley Stories series for girls ages 10 to 13.

Find more fun books at:
www.CrimsonHillBooks.com

Photo Credits

Thank you to:

Shutterstock: Siarhei Kasilau, Matt Jeppson, Lauren Suryanata, Kuznetsov Alexey, Dan Olsen, RAY Photographer, Mike Wilhelm, reptile4all, Karit Afshen, Jay Ondreicka, KF2017, Milan Rybar and Lauren Suryanata

Pixabay: Karsten Paulick, Vicki Hamilton, Amandad, Eliza, Justin Smith, Linh Hoang, Obaid Rehman, Gundula Vogel, Foto-Rabe, Michael Kleinsasser, Storme, Silvia, Istvan, Rey Movida, Haim Charbit, Storme, Vandy Louw, Antriksh Kuman, Alexander Lesnitsky, Dezalb, Marc Pascval, Paul Brennan, Badrudin, Petr Ganaj, Taskin Ahmed, Alan Wooler, Lukasz Ziomek, Jacky Barrit, Mrs. Kirk, Katy Heejin, Pixl1, Pam Carter, 127071, Kev, Bex, Mark Pascual, Peter Woelfel, Don, Sipa, Makeitsomarketing, Haruko Tobata, Vieleineinerhuelle, Badrudin, Margaret Saldais, Yuri B, Ziomek, Alexandra Lysenko, Theresa McGee, CDPHOTOGRAPHY, Rey Modiva and Denis Doukhan

Wikimedia: safaritravelplus, Tim Vickers, Q Phia

Flickr: Barry Kiepe

and also illustrators Daniel Eskridge and Prokhorovich.

Loved all these great facts and photos? Discover MORE about your favourite pets and animals in these books:

- **Fun Leopard Gecko and Bearded Dragon Facts for Kids**
- **Fun Reptile Facts for Kids**
- **Fun Dog Facts for Kids**
- **Fun Cat Facts for Kids**
- **Fun Pony Facts for Kids**
- **Fun Horse Facts for Kids**
- **Fun Bird Facts for Kids**
- **Fun Backyard Bird Facts for Kids**
- **Fun Dinosaur Facts for Kids**
- **Fun T-Rex Facts for Kids**
- **Fun Snake Facts for Kids**
- **Fun Bug Facts for Kids**
- **Fun Spider Facts for Kids**

www.ingramcontent.com/pod-product-compliance
Lightning Source LLC
Chambersburg PA
CBHW071113120626
46546CB00003B/1323